Easter Riddles and Trick Questions
for Kids & Family!

Hundreds of Riddles
and Brain Teasers
That Kids and Family Will Enjoy!

With
Fun Illustrations

Riddleland

D1416111

Table of Contents

Bonus

Riddleland Bonus

Join our **Facebook Group** at **Riddleland for Kids** to get daily jokes and riddles.

Bonus Book

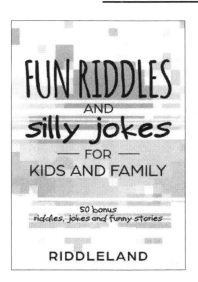

https://pixelfy.me/riddlelandbonus

Thank you for buying this book. As a token of our appreciation, we would like to offer a special bonus—a collection of 50 original jokes, riddles, and funny stories.

Introduction

"Egg hunts are proof that your children can find things when they really want"
~ Unknown

We would like to personally thank you for purchasing this book. **Easter Riddles and Trick Questions for Kids and Family** is a collection of fun brain teasers and riddles of easy to hard difficulty.

These brain teasers will challenge children and their parents to think and stretch their minds. They also have many other benefits such as:

- **Bonding** – It is an excellent way for parents and their children to spend some quality time and create some fun and memorable memories.

- **Confidence Building** - When parents ask the riddles, it creates a safe environment for children to burst out answers even if they are incorrect. This helps children to develop self-confidence in expressing themselves.

- **Improve Vocabulary** – Riddles are usually written in advanced words, therefore children will need to understand these words before they can share the riddles.

• **Better reading comprehension** – Many children can read at a young age but may not understand the context of the sentences. Riddles can help develop children's interest to comprehend the context before they can share the riddles with their friends

• **Sense of humor** – Funny creative riddles can help children develop their sense of humor while getting their brains working.

Chapter : 1

Easy Riddles

"A true friend is someone who thinks you're a good egg, even if you're cracked."

1. The Easter bunny found a green egg floating down the green river. Where on earth did the egg come from?

2. I am the symbol of hope; I literally make the darkness of winter disappear and the days be longer. My Egyptian name was Ra, and a day of the week is named in my honor.

What am I?

3. What do you have to hunt down and break apart before you can eat it?

4. Do you know how many Easter eggs you can put into an empty Easter egg basket?

5. I am orange, but I'm not an orange. I am bunny food. My name rhymes with parrot, but Polly doesn't want me because I'm not a cracker.

What am I?

6. I am the color of the first Easter egg. People wanted the egg to stand out from the other eggs, so they painted it the same color used on many firetrucks and stop signs today.

What color am I?

Chapter 1 - Questions

7. What stories are the Easter bunny's favorite stories?

8. Can you name the three treats that you always have on Easter day?

9. There are ten Easter eggs on the ground. If you take away two, then how many Easter eggs do you have?

10. What is always wet and can't get any wetter than it is, comes down but can't go up, and is seen all the time around spring and Easter time?

11. In the winter people pour water over me to make a hot beverage; at Easter I can be found wrapped in foil in the shape of an egg or a bunny.

What am I?

12. The Easter bunny hid three Easter eggs behind the big bush outside, he hid two in the flowerpot by the door, he hid ten along the fence around the house, and he hid one underneath your pillow. How many Easter eggs did the Easter bunny hide?

Chapter 1 - Questions

13. Why do people believe bunnies have really good eyesight?

14. There really is a place called Easter Island, and it is part of me. I am a South American country. Some people say my name sounds like a bowl of stew; other people say that it sounds like the opposite of warm.

What is my name?

15. What name would you give to a group of bunnies hopping backward together?

FUN FACT

Have a guess at how many Cadbury's Creme Eggs are made each day? 1.5 million!!!! There are over 500 million Creme Eggs made each year, and if they were stacked in a column, they'd be ten times higher than Mount Everest !

Chapter 1 - Questions

16. The White House Easter Egg Roll tradition began in 1878 when I was President. My last name sounds like I lived in a fog, but don't let that fool you.

Who am I?

17. Do you know what the Easter bunny's favorite day is?

18. What day does the Easter bunny hate the most out of all the days?

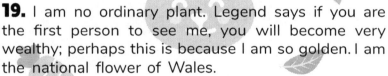

19. I am no ordinary plant. Legend says if you are the first person to see me, you will become very wealthy; perhaps this is because I am so golden. I am the national flower of Wales.

What am I?

20. Do you know what is red and blue, and can make a huge mess in the bottom of your Easter basket?

21. What would you call a funny book about Easter eggs?

22. What would you get if you mixed a chicken with a Chihuahua?

23. Why was the Easter bunny rubbing the sides of his head?

24. What should you say to everyone on Easter day?

25. I am the sacred goddess of spring. My sacred animal was the rabbit and my symbol for rebirth was the egg. I walked around carrying a woven basket in the crook of my arm, the first Easter basket. Remember that the day dawns in the East, and keep in mind that my name reflects this dawning of new life.

Who am I?

26. Why was the Easter bunny so upset?

27. Do you know how Easter ends?

FUN FACT

How big do you think the largest Easter egg is? The largest Easter egg is in Alberta, Canada. It weighs 5000lbs, is 3ft tall, and 18 ft wide. It has a name, it's called the Vegreville Pysanka.

28. When Easter happens, I am full - but I have not eaten. Although I am around in the day, most people see me only at night.

What am I?

29. Where did the Easter bunny hide his Easter eggs before the Easter Island was discovered?

30. Medieval Easter eggs were boiled with me to give them a bright shine. I have lots of rings, but I am not a jeweler. I am known for bringing tears to people's eyes. What am I?

31. The Easter bunny manages to paint all of the Easter eggs, but he doesn't do it by himself. Do you know the Easter bunny's secret method?

32. I am a flower that symbolizes rebirth. My white color reflects purity. My trumpet shape announces spring has arrived. The fact that I began life buried and then came to life reminds people of rebirth.

What is my name?

33. I am the second most popular Easter Game; the Easter egg hunt is the most popular. To win my game, you must roll your egg the furthest without breaking it.

What is my name?

34. Mr. Turtle asked the Easter bunny if he wanted to race, and even though he was busy, the Easter bunny said yes. Who won the race?

35. Who travels faster: the Easter bunny or the tooth fairy?

36. I made the world's first bar in 1847 and, 28 years later in 1873, I made the world's first chocolate Easter egg. I was an English candy maker, and my name is still associated with candy in England today. To hear my name, you would think I am just a regular Joe; in fact, my last name sounds so silly it may remind you of a French fried potato.

Who am I?

Chapter 1 - Questions

37. Why did the Easter bunny get stuck trying to climb through the window?

38. Easter is so awesome! I love the eggs, the chocolate, the flowers, the rain, and the Easter bunny. What a nice sentence. Can you spell it without using the letter 'S?'

39. I represent the end of a long hard winter. A chicken breaks out of me, reminding people of new life. Together, the chicken and I remind people that no matter how bad things look, there is hope.

What am I?

40. What color are the feathers on the Easter bunny's chickens?

41. What does the Easter bunny eat for breakfast?

42. One of the Easter bunny's assistants went outside without an umbrella, jacket, hat, or hood but not a strand of fur on his body got wet.

How is this possible?

43. What can you find at the very center of an Easter bunny?

44. What has to be broken open before you can actually use it?

45. Why did the Easter bunny tell the Easter eggs to lose some weight?

46. What is the Easter bunny's favorite game to play?

47. I am one of the four seasons. I come before summer and after winter. Easter is one of my holidays. My name may remind you of a wire coil.

What am I?

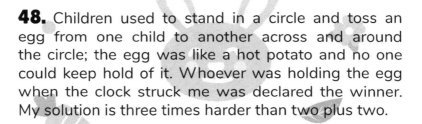

48. Children used to stand in a circle and toss an egg from one child to another across and around the circle; the egg was like a hot potato and no one could keep hold of it. Whoever was holding the egg when the clock struck me was declared the winner. My solution is three times harder than two plus two.

What is my name?

49. I am hidden really well but you can find me if you are willing to look some more. I am tasty, colorful, and small but don't drop me on the floor. If you drop me, I will break, and you won't be able to taste me. It's not just me because my many brothers and sisters are exactly the same. Do you know our name?

FUN FACT

How much money do you think an Easter egg costs? In 2007 an Easter egg sold for £9 million (that's approx. $11,875,500.00). It was a gold and pink enamelled egg containing a cockerel that each hour came out of the egg and flapped his wings and nodded his head. It was made by Karl Faberge in St Petersburg in 1902.

Chapter 1 - Questions

50. The White House Easter Egg Roll/Hunt did not begin at the White House; it occurred on the Capital lawn a few years before changing venues. William Holman, an Indiana representative, wrote a bill and got it passed making it illegal to have the Easter egg hunt on the lawn – and he did it all in the name of saving me!

What am I?

51. If it takes one chicken five minutes to paint an Easter egg how long will it take two chickens to paint half an Easter egg?

52. What is the first thing everyone does on Easter morning?

53. I am known for not only dyeing Easter eggs but also delivering the eggs and hiding them on lawns and in houses on the evening before Easter. Some people place a carrot on the lawn so that I know in what part of the yard to hide the eggs.

Who am I?

54. Can you tell me what came first: the chicken or the egg?

55. Today in America marshmallow Peeps come in a variety of animal shapes and flavors. I am the original marshmallow Peep; try to guess my shape and color. To look at my color, you might think I was jaundiced or cowardly. Next, take one look at my shape and you will know that with me talk is 'cheep.'

What am I?

56. Why is the Easter bunny always happy when it is a leap year?

57. What kind of music is the Easter bunny's favorite?

58. I am the country where the Easter Bunny originated; he was first seen hiding eggs in 1680. I am in Europe and am one of the countries comprising the European Union. My people are healthy, but my name may remind you of sickness. Speaking of language, if you say that you want nine eggs in my country, you might get none, because "nine" means none in my country's language.

FUN FACT

Do you know how many jellybeans are eaten in the US at Easter? 16 million. That's enough jellybeans to go round the earth three times!

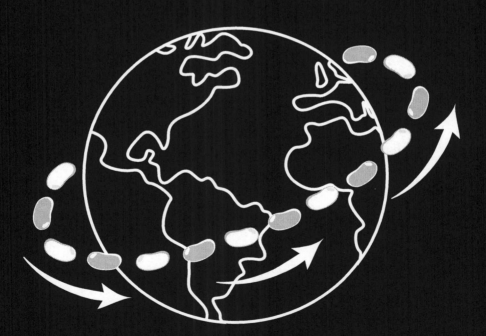

59. What is the Easter bunny's favorite hiding spot for his Easter eggs?

60. What do the bunnies and chickens on Easter Island use for money?

61. What happened to the Easter Island heads' bodies?

62. Although I hatch from a chicken egg, I will never grow up to lay an Easter egg – or any egg for that matter.

What am I?

63. How did the Easter bunny manage to stay fit even though he eats so many chocolate eggs?

64. Do you know why the Easter bunny started feeding his chickens crayons?

65. Rabbits are really good at math. Do you know why?

66. What did the Easter bunny say to the carrot?

67. Why did the Easter egg hide away? Why didn't he want to be found?

68. What should you feed a dog on Easter day?

69. One of the Easter bunny's assistants is known only as Hop the Bunny. What is Hop the Bunny's middle name?

Chapter 1 - Questions

70. Why are 2020 Easter eggs worth a lot more than 1990 Easter eggs?

71. Can you tell me why people are always tired when April comes around?

72. Which rabbits are the oldest rabbits in the group?

73. What do you call the Easter bunny when he has fleas?

74. Lots of people, particularly children, receive chocolate bunnies as an Easter treat. I am the part of the bunny that is most likely to be consumed first by the majority of people. If you have anything to say to me, you had better say it now.

What am I?

75. What kind of music does the Easter bunny's band play?

76. Do you know why the Easter bunny was forced to fire the duck?

Chapter 1 - Questions

77. What name do you give to a really smart bunny?

78. Don't let me pull the wool over your eyes. I am an animal associated with spring. In fact, March typically comes in like a lion, but it goes out as me.

What am I?

79. What happens when you cross the Easter bunny with a bee?

80. What kind of phone does the Easter bunny have?

81. Who hides eggs on Easter day in the sea for the fish?

82. What sport does the Easter bunny like to play when he is on a break?

FUN FACT

Do you know what flower is connected to Easter? The white lily, which represents grace and purity. They're known as 'Easter lilies'.

Chapter 1 - Questions

83. Why didn't the bunny want to hop?

84. What does the Easter bunny do when it is raining?

85. What would you call an egg that came from outer space?

86. What kind of bunnies don't know how to hop?

87. What does the Easter bunny do if his chickens aren't laying eggs and he needs eggs to hide before Easter day?

88. In 1290, King Edward I of England had 450 Easter eggs dipped in me and distributed to his friends. Today, a medal made of me is often given to first place finishers.

What am I?

89. Why are bunnies the luckiest animals in the world?

90. How does the Easter bunny make sure he doesn't get lost while hiding eggs in the woods?

91. I am the most popular game associated with Easter; the egg roll is the second most popular. My game also involves eggs - hard boiled dyed eggs that are scattered around the room/lawn.

What is my name?

Chapter 1 - Questions

92. Do you know why the fox ran across the road?

93. You'll find it mostly at Easter, but it shows up at Christmas, too. It shows up a lot on Valentine's Day.

What is it?

94. I am the original Easter basket. In the first part of my life, I held real eggs, now I hold chocolate eggs and dyed eggs. I was created by winged creatures, but these were not angels.

What am I?

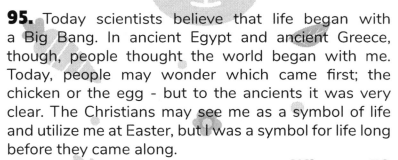

95. Today scientists believe that life began with a Big Bang. In ancient Egypt and ancient Greece, though, people thought the world began with me. Today, people may wonder which came first; the chicken or the egg - but to the ancients it was very clear. The Christians may see me as a symbol of life and utilize me at Easter, but I was a symbol for life long before they came along.

What am I?

96. I am one of two colors traditionally associated with Easter. Whereas my counterpart purple reflects majesty, I reflect brightness and joy. (Ignore those people who say that I represent cowards.)

What color am I?

FUN FACT

How do you eat chocolate bunnies? More than ¾ of all people asked, bite the ears off first. A smaller proportion start at the feet, and an even smaller amount of people bite the tail first.

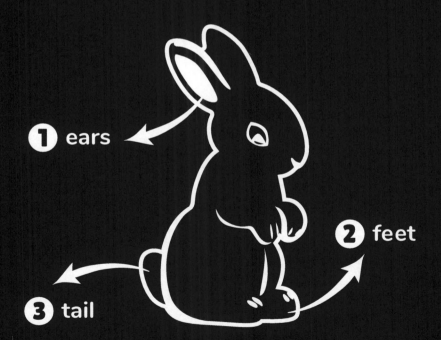

1 ears

2 feet

3 tail

97. If a bunny had a baby with a frog what would it be called?

98. What is it called when chickens are playing games?

Chapter 1 - Answers

1. The egg must have come from a chicken of course.

2. The sun; that day of the week, of course, is Sunday.

3. An Easter egg!

4. You can only put one Easter egg into a basket, after that it won't be empty anymore.

5. A carrot.

6. Red.

7. Stories with hoppy (happy) endings, of course.

8. Chocolate eggs, hot cross buns, and a glass of milk.

9. You have only two eggs: the two that you took.

10. The rain!

11. Chocolate

12. He hid 16 eggs!

13. Because no one has ever seen a bunny wearing glasses

14. Chile.

15. A receding hare-line.

16. Rutherford Hayes.

17. The day before Easter is his favorite day because that's when he gets to hide all of the eggs.

18. The day after Easter

19. Daffodil

20. Broken Easter eggs, of course.

21. A yolk book!

22. You get pooched eggs!

23. He had an egg-ache (headache).

24. Hoppy Easter!

25. Eastre.

26. Because he was having a bad hare day.

27. With the letter "R"

28. Moon.

29. The Easter bunny hides his eggs in parks, gardens, and houses. The Easter bunny doesn't hide his eggs on Easter Island; that's only where he keeps his factory.

30. Onion

31. He hires Santa's workers to help him during the off-season.

Chapter 1 - Answers

32. Easter Lily.

33. Egg roll

34. Answer: The Easter bunny won, of course! The Easter bunny can hide millions of eggs all around the world in one night; he wouldn't lose a race to a turtle.

35. The Easter bunny is faster because he manages to deliver all his eggs all around the world in one night. The tooth fairy only picks up a few teeth a night.

36. Joseph Fry

37. Because he was too fat to fit.

---

38. I.T. It's not that difficult to spell without the letter 'S.'

39. Egg shell.

40. Brown! All of the Easter bunny's chickens are made of chocolate so their feathers are obviously brown.

41. Hot cross buns, what else?

42. I didn't say that it was raining.

43. A heart made of chocolate!

44. An egg, of course.

45. Because they were getting too heavy to carry!

46. Hide and seek with his eggs!

47. Spring

48. Twelve

---

49. Easter egg is our name and hiding is our game.

50. Grass. Holman believed having people on the lawn would ruin it.

51. Have you ever seen an Easter egg that's only half painted? The Easter bunny would never allow only half an egg to be painted!

52. Get out of bed!

53. Easter Bunny Rabbit

54. I'm pretty sure the dinosaurs were laying eggs long before chickens were.

55. A yellow chicken.

56. Because that means he gets an extra day to get his eggs ready for Easter.

57. Hip-hop, of course!

Chapter 1 - Answers

58. Germany.

59. In his stomach!

60. They use chocolate coins and chocolate chips!

61. Nobody knows! Do you get the joke?

62. A rooster.

63. When the Easter bunny's not hiding eggs or eating them, he is Egg-xercising!

64. He wanted them to lay eggs that were already colored!

---

65. Because they're really good at multiplying!

66. He said, "It was nice gnawing you."

67. Because he was a little chicken!

68. A jelly bone, of course.

69. 'The.' Hop the Bunny's middle name is 'the.'

70. Because there are more of them! 2020 is a bigger number than 1990, so 2020 Easter eggs are worth more than 1990 Easter eggs because there are more of them.

71. Because they just came out of a March.

72. The ones with grey hairs!

---

73. Bugs Bunny!

74. The ears.

75. Hip-hop, of course.

76. He had to fire the duck because the duck kept quacking all the Easter eggs.

77. We call him an egghead!

78. Lamb.

79. You get a honey bunny

80. An I-hop-phone.

81. The oyster bunny!

82. Basketball, of course.

83. No bunny knows.

84. He gets wet! What else can he do?

Chapter 1 - Answers

85. An Egg-stra-terrestrial.

86. Chocolate bunnies!

87. He gets his eggs from an eggplant!

88. Gold (technically gold leaf)

89. Because they have four lucky rabbit's feet.

90. He follows the trail of eggs he leaves behind.

91. Easter Egg Hunt.

---

92. Because he was chasing the chicken.

93. It's chocolate! Chocolate eggs, to be precise.

94. A bird's nest.

95. The egg.

96. Yellow.

97. A bunny ribbit of course.

98. Fowl (foul) play.

Chapter : 2

Hard Riddles

"There are always flowers for those
who want to see them."

~ Henri Matisse

Chapter 2 - Questions

1. What is as big as the Easter bunny but doesn't weigh as much as the Easter bunny?

2. What is fluffy, white, and travels around the world day and night?

3. How many days are there in Easter?

Chapter 2 - Questions

4. If the Easter bunny was the one laying all of the Easter eggs what color would his feathers be?

5. I don't have any special powers, but I can tell you where all of the Easter eggs are hidden.

Who am I?

6. I am a word that most soldiers hate to hear. I am also a month. Easter either falls in me or in my buddy, April. Unlike my other neighbor February which may have 28 or 29 days, you can always count on me to have 31 days.

What is my name?

7. The Easter bunny is busy counting all his Easter eggs to make sure he has enough for Easter. He has reached 300 eggs and he has written them all down on a page. When he starts a new page, he will need to count from 300 eggs to 400 eggs on that page. How many times will he have to write the number 3?

8. Can you name a word that has only four letters but comes in dozens?

9. I am warm, round, and brown. I taste the best because I am so sweet! With an edible cross on top, I am a really tasty treat.

What am I?

10. It is just a head, sitting on the ground with nothing to do. It doesn't move and it doesn't speak. It's just a head on the ground with nothing underneath. Do you know what it is?

11. Why doesn't the Easter bunny hide his eggs underneath the Christmas tree?

FUN FACT

Do you know where the name
Easter comes from? Eostre
an Anglo-Saxon goddess,
connected to light, dawn and
celebrating spring.

Chapter 2 - Questions

12. I am a bread with raisins or currants. I am typically served on Good Friday; I am known for my icing which is in the shape of crosses.

What am I?

13. I am a salty pastry treat. I was created to remind people to pray; people say I look like a person with folded arms. I am knotty, not naughty. I am one long string of dough that has been intertwined and then twisted back on itself. I have been around since 300-600.

What am I?

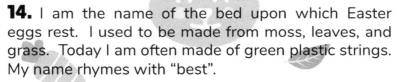

14. I am the name of the bed upon which Easter eggs rest. I used to be made from moss, leaves, and grass. Today I am often made of green plastic strings. My name rhymes with "best".

What am I?

15. If you look you will find two in Easter and you'll find three in Easter eggs. You won't find it at all in Christmas, but you will see two of them in presents. The tooth fairy doesn't have one, but teeth have two

What is it?

16. Do you know what you'll find in the middle of Easter Island?

Chapter 2 - Questions

17. The Easter bunny is having some friends over and he needs 7 gallons of milk for them all to drink. You have a 5-gallon jar and a 3-gallon jar. How can you measure out 7 gallons of milk for the Easter bunny using only these two jars?

18. The Easter bunny is playing with his friend Jim. The Easter bunny only has three friends that he plays with and they're all ducks. Their names are Huey, Duey, and...? Do you know the third friend's name is?

19. I am home to over 1,500 Easter eggs year-round. I am the largest museum devoted to Easter eggs. I am found in the country of Poland.

What is my name?

20. I am named after the queen of England, Victoria. During my time, it became acceptable to give chocolates and other candy on Easter. What age am I (it's not a number, it relates to an era)?

21. I am the network of underground interconnecting burrows in which rabbits live. My name may remind you of the piece of paper a police officer needs to conduct a search in the United States. I am the hole-thing.

What is my name?

22. A little girl found a dozen Easter eggs hidden in the park. On her way home, she dropped the eggs and all but three cracked. How many eggs does she have left that are unbroken?

23. I know a word that is made up of only six letters. If you take one letter away, then you will be left with twelve. What word is it that I know? Hint: It's often used to describe a number of eggs.

Chapter 2 - Questions

24. This thing comes in many shapes and sizes. It can be dark, brown, or white. Whatever its shape, size, or color it is always eaten with delight.

What is it?

25. The Easter bunny was hiding eggs near the beach when a thief ran past and took one of the eggs. The Easter bunny chased after the thief, but he was smaller and faster than the poor bunny. The Easter bunny followed the thief to the beach, but then he lost him. The Easter bunny looked around and found a way to follow the thief. He found the thief hidden in a cave and took the stolen egg back. How was the Easter bunny able to find the thief?

26. Everyone knows bunnies eat carrots, but the Easter bunny eats chocolate carrots. He likes to eat chocolate carrots for lunch but each day he eats twice as many carrots as he ate the day before. If he ate 2 carrots on Monday, then how many carrots would he have eaten by Sunday?

27. The Easter bunny is exactly 5 times as old as his dog, Fluffy, is. The Easter bunny is 30 years old. How old is Fluffy?

28. If it takes four jellybeans to make a single Easter egg, how many jellybeans do you need to make 40 Easter eggs?

29. The Easter bunny has an egg problem. It's the day before Easter and all of the chickens are laying giant jellybeans instead of Easter eggs. Someone fed them jellybeans instead of chocolate. How can the Easter bunny fix this egg problem?

30. I live inside a little house. My house has no doors and no windows and the only way for me to get out is if I break through the walls of my house.

What am I?

FUN FACT

Do you know where painting Easter eggs originated? They came from Ukraine, it is called pysanka, and eggs were painted using wax and dyes.

Chapter 2 - Questions

31. What does Easter Island and the letter 'T' have in common?

32. The Easter bunny has a big family. He has 20 sons and each of his sons has a sister. How many children does the Easter bunny have?

33. It rained nonstop on Easter day but that didn't stop people from looking for Easter eggs. Even though it was raining all day, none of the Easter eggs got wet during the egg hunt. How is this possible?

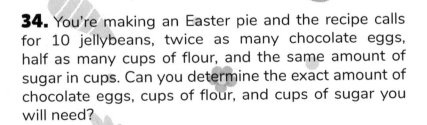

34. You're making an Easter pie and the recipe calls for 10 jellybeans, twice as many chocolate eggs, half as many cups of flour, and the same amount of sugar in cups. Can you determine the exact amount of chocolate eggs, cups of flour, and cups of sugar you will need?

35. The Easter bunny is covered in bunny fur. He has a unique sweater that is made from the wool of a unique sheep. What color is the Easter bunny's sweater?

36. The Easter bunny's assistant was looking at some old photos of the Easter bunny and he came across one photo with two people in it, a young bunny and an older bunny. He asked the Easter bunny who was in the photo and the Easter bunny replied, "I have no brothers or sisters, but that bunny's father is my father's son." Do you know who is in the photo?

37. The Easter bunny and his assistant were going for a walk outside and they saw a field that was full of bunnies. When they looked again the field didn't have a single bunny in it. How is this possible?

38. How many strokes of the paint brush does it take to finish painting an Easter egg?

39. Some of the Easter bunny's kids were playing down by the lake. There were three of them and they were playing tag! The bunnies ran into each other and all three of them fell into the lake. Two of them got wet but not a single piece of fur on the third got wet. How is this possible?

Chapter 2 - Questions

40. There are 10 Easter eggs on the kitchen counter. You take away 5 of them. How many do you have?

41. You can call me the Easter Rabbit or the Easter Bunny, but my original name was neither "rabbit" or "bunny". Think carefully; you could be fooled by a hair. Can you think of my full original name?

42. I am a sugary candy that has a chewy center. I was a popular penny candy around 1900 and, beginning in the 1930s I became associated with Easter because of my egg shape. I come in a variety of colors and flavors.

What am I?

43. I am the last day of the carnival season, and sometimes I am called Carnival Carnival Carnival. I am held the day before Lent begins, giving everyone one last chance to have a good time before the somber time of self-reflection. I feature parades, public street parties, and circus elements. Many people are dressed in very elaborate masks. I am French for "Fat Tuesday".

What am I?

Chapter 2 - Questions

44. What doesn't belong on this list: eggs, chocolate, jellybeans, goats, bunnies, chickens, ducks, flowers, and rain?

45. The Easter bunny was in the middle of his afternoon snack when his assistant came by and asked him what he was eating. "I am eating Chinese gooseberries," the Easter bunny told him. "Where are they from?" asked his assistant. "They're not from China," is the only thing the Easter bunny said.

Do you know where Chinese gooseberries are from?

FUN FACT

Have you noticed your Easter eggs/candy disappear faster than you expected? 81% of parents have admitted to taking sweets/chocolate from their children's Easter haul.

Easter Egg

Chapter 2 - Questions

46. The Easter bunny is getting ready for Easter. He must make sure that all his workers are at the factory but there are so many of them he can't count them out one at a time. He decided to have them all stand in the same room. He counted the ears of all the bunnies and counted all the feet of the chickens. There were 50 ears in the room and 70 feet in the room. How many chickens and bunnies were in the room?

47. The Easter bunny loves his pets and has got so many of them. His latest pet is a purple finch. Do you know what color his finch is?

48. If five bunnies can eat five Easter eggs in five minutes, then how many Easter eggs can twenty bunnies eat in twenty minutes?

49. If two days from now I told you that the day before yesterday was Easter, then what day is today?

50. I am a box, a cage. I typically have a wire mesh front. I am where domesticated rabbits, as well as ferrets and similar animals, call home.

What am I?

Chapter 2 - Questions

51. There was a beautiful sunset and the Easter bunny wanted to take a picture of it. He ran and got his camera, but when he got back, he wasn't in the right position to take the perfect photo. The Easter bunny turned left, then he turned right, then he spun all around, he did a handstand and a backflip, walked five steps back and took the perfect picture of the sunset. In which direction was the Easter bunny facing when he took the picture?

52. The Easter bunny takes many tools with him to help him hide all the Easter eggs. One of the things he always takes with him when he is going to places like New York City, and other places with big buildings, is an umbrella. Why does the Easter bunny need an umbrella to help him in these places?

53. The Easter bunny was sitting in the car as his assistant drove him to the last three houses on the street. Normally the Easter bunny doesn't drive, but he was running out of time and had to move quickly before Easter day. He only has three houses left to hide Easter eggs in. Then he will be done for the night. One house has a blue door, the other house has a green door, and the third house has a yellow door. Which door should the Easter bunny open first?

54. I am 46 days before Easter. Many people give up something for the entire period, many others simply give up meat on Friday. My name sounds as if I was borrowed, but I am actually the Old English word for "spring".

What am I?

55. To win a traditional Easter egg hunt, you must find more eggs than anyone else finds. In modern times people often limit the number of eggs each person can find, so, to be declared winner, you must find me, the extra special egg. I am named after a precious metal.

What is my name?

56. These things can be hollow and made of chocolate on the inside, or they could be the real deal and painted on the outside.

What are they?

Chapter 2 - Questions

57. Many people fast during Lent, that is, they give up food or something they really like. Lent begins with Ash Wednesday and runs until Easter. Therefore, on the Tuesday before that Wednesday, many people want to use up their leftovers, such as extra pancake batter, before the fasting begins. Meanwhile, other people choose to celebrate, gorging themselves on luxuries they will deprive themselves of on days ahead. This Tuesday celebration is known as Mardi Gras, Shrove Tuesday, Pancake Day and my name, a reminder that people are storing food for lean times to come.

What am I called?

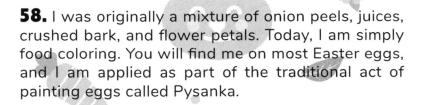

58. I was originally a mixture of onion peels, juices, crushed bark, and flower petals. Today, I am simply food coloring. You will find me on most Easter eggs, and I am applied as part of the traditional act of painting eggs called Pysanka.

What am I?

59. The Easter bunny's hens lay two eggs every hour. If the first egg they lay in an hour is blue, then what are the odds that the second egg they lay is also blue?

60. The Easter bunny was out hiding eggs in the rain. When he got home, he was soaked to the bone. How did the Easter bunny dry his wet fur?

61. I am the circular cake used to remind people that the Wise Men took a different route back to their land rather than go back through Jerusalem. Inside me you will find a bean or other token; the person who gets the token gets the honor of making me next year. Some people serve me on the first day of the carnival season, i.e., Epiphany, while others wait until the very last day, Mardi Gras.

What am I?

62. The Easter bunny was walking towards another bunny. This bunny looked exactly like him and seemed to be walking exactly like him as well. They walked closer to each other and eventually bumped right into each other. Can you explain what just happened?

63. If vampires use blood money and the fish keep their money in a riverbank, then what kind of money does the Easter bunny use and where does he keep it?

64. There are four types of chocolate: blonde, milk, white, and me. I was the chocolate used in the first chocolate egg made by John Cadbury's company in 1875.

What am I?

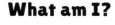

FUN FACT

Do you know what people do in Norway over the Easter weekend? They read crime stories. This dates back to 1923 when authors promoted their new crime novel on the front page of a newspaper, and people thought it was true. Their novel became hugely successful.

NEWS

New Crime Novel by XXX author

1923 year

chapter 1 crime story

Chapter 2 - Answers

1. The Easter bunny's shadow!

2. The clouds! You said, 'the Easter bunny,' didn't you?

3. There's only one day in Easter and that's Easter day.

4. He wouldn't have feathers because he is a bunny. He has fur!

5. I am the Easter bunny. I know where the eggs are because I hid them.

6. March.

7. He'll write the number 3 zero times. He is writing numbers from 300 to 400 so he has already passed the number 3. He will write numbers with 3 in them like 333 but that isn't the number 3 that is the number 333.

8. Eggs

9. I am a hot cross bun.

10. It is a head statue from Easter Island.

11. He can't because the Christmas tree won't be up on Easter.

12. Hot cross buns.

13. A pretzel.

14. Nest.

15. It is the letter 'E.'

16. A space! Both the words Easter and Island have six letters, so the space used to separate the words is right in the middle.

17. First you must fill the 5-gallon jar completely then pour from the 5-gallon jar into the 3-gallon jar until it is full. This will leave two gallons in the 5-gallon jar. Now empty the 3-gallon jar. Pour the remaining 2 gallons of milk that is in the 5-gallon jar into the now empty 3-gallon jar. Lastly, fill the 5-gallon jar again. Now you have 7 gallons of milk; 5 gallons in the 5-gallon jar and 2 gallons in the 3-gallon jar.

Chapter 2 - Answers

18. The third friend's name is Jim! The Easter bunny was playing with him.

19. Easter Egg Museum.

20. Victorian Age/Era.

21. Warren.

22. She has three unbroken eggs. She had a dozen, which is 12, but then she broke all but three of them. She has three eggs left.

23. 'Dozens' is the word you're looking for. There are six letters in the word but if you take away the 'S' at the end you'll be left with 'dozen' which is another word for 12.

24. It is chocolate!

25. The Easter bunny was on a beach, so he was able to follow the footprints the thief left behind in the sand.

26. He would have eaten 254 chocolate carrots by Sunday. If he ate 2 on Monday, then on Tuesday he would have eaten 4, on Wednesday he would have eaten 8, and so on.

27. To find the answer to this question we need to take the Easter bunny's age and divide it by five. If he is five times older than his dog, then 30 divided by 5 equals 6. His dog is 6 years old.

28. You need 160 jellybeans to make 40 Easter eggs. You can figure this out by taking the number of Easter eggs you need and multiplying that number by the number of jellybeans it takes to make one Easter egg. 40 multiplied by 4 equals 160.

29. The Easter bunny can start feeding the chicken lots of chocolate, so they start laying lots of chocolate eggs just in time for Easter.

Chapter 2 - Answers

30. I am a baby chicken in an egg.

31. They're both in the middle of water! Easter Island is in the middle of water because it's an island, and the letter 'T' is in the middle of the word 'water.'

32. The Easter bunny has 21 children. He has 20 sons and one daughter.

33. None of the eggs got wet because all of them were hidden inside a house!

34. The recipe calls for 10 jellybeans, twice as many chocolate eggs, half as many cups of flour, and the same amount of sugar in cups. The only measuring number we've been given is 10 for the jellybeans, so we have to use that number to calculate the rest. Twice as many chocolate eggs means twice the amount of the 10 jellybeans, so we need 20 chocolate eggs. Half as many cups of flour means half the amount of 10 jellybeans but in cups, so we need 5 cups of flour. The same amount of sugar in cups means we need the same amount of 10 jellybeans but in cups, so we need 10 cups of sugar. That's a very sweet pie!

35. The Easter bunny's sweater is black! A unique sheep would be a black sheep because there are less black sheep than there are white sheep.

36. The Easter bunny and his son are in the photo. When he says that bunny's father is my father's son, he is talking about himself. He is his father's son, and he is the bunny's father.

37. All the bunnies in the field are in a relationship. Therefore, none of them were single.

38. Just one stroke. The last stroke of the paintbrush and the egg is finished.

Chapter 2 - Answers

39. One of the bunnies was hairless!

40. You have five of them (the five that you took).

41. Easter Hare.

42. Jelly Bean

43. Mardi Gras.

44. 'Goats' doesn't belong on the list. The list is filled with things connected to Easter and 'goats' do not belong.

45. Chinese gooseberries come from New Zealand.

46. There are 25 bunnies and 35 chickens in the room. You can figure this out by dividing the number of ears and the number of feet by 2. 50 divided by 2 is 25 and 70 divided by 2 is 35. You do this because each bunny will have 2 ears and each chicken will have 2 feet.

47. A purple finch is usually a crimson color.

48. 20 Easter eggs! If it takes five minutes for five bunnies to eat five Easter eggs, then that means they are each eating an Easter egg a minute. It will be the same for 20 bunnies in 20 minutes. They'll eat one egg each a minute. They'll eat 20 eggs in total.

49. Today is Easter! Two days from now, the 'day before yesterday' will be today. Therefore, today is Easter.

50. Hutch

51. The Easter bunny was taking a picture of the sunset and the sun sets in the west. He had to have been facing west.

Chapter 2 - Answers

52. The buildings are so tall that the Easter bunny is too short to reach all the buttons in the elevator. He especially can't reach the buttons that lead to the top floor. He takes the umbrella with him so he can use it to reach the buttons.

53. The car door

54. Lent.

55. The Golden Egg

56. They're Easter Eggs!

57. Fat Tuesday.

58. Easter egg dye.

59. Exactly fifty percent. If you are figuring out the odds of one outcome occurring, and the problem only has two possible outcomes, the odds will always work out at 50 percent. 50 percent for the one and 50 percent for the other.

60. He used a hare-dryer!

61. King Cake.

62. The Easter bunny was walking towards a mirror.

63. The Easter bunny uses chocolate coins as money, and he keeps them in his tummy!

64. Dark chocolate.

Chapter : 3

Difficult Riddles

"Easter is the only time when it's perfectly safe to put all of your eggs in one basket"

~ Evan Esar

Chapter 3 - Questions

1. The Easter bunny's assistant was busy putting away the eggs one night. He had 300 eggs to put away. 10 of them got up and ran away from him, 20 fell out of his hands and rolled away, and 50 of them found a place to hide and wouldn't come out. How many eggs does the Easter bunny's assistant have left to put away?

2. Imagine that the Easter bunny has asked you to help him hide the Easter eggs. He gives you a basket filled with enough eggs for one house. You must hide all the eggs and you can't lose any of them. You place an egg on the ground to hide it, but it rolls away from you and disappears down a drain. You don't want the Easter bunny to be angry with you because you lost one of the eggs, so how can you fix the situation?

3. It's late at night and all your Easter eggs have been stolen by a thief. You're chasing him around the woods but it's very dark and you can't see him. The thief can see perfectly in the dark. The good thing is the thief can only go around in circles, but you can run wherever you want. How can you catch the thief and get your eggs back without being able to see him or know where he is going?

4. The Easter bunny threw a party and invited all his bunny and chicken friends. He asked every bunny coming to the party to bring five Easter eggs and he asked every chicken coming to the party to bring two glasses of milk. When everyone had arrived, he had 50 Easter eggs and 20 glasses of milk. How many bunnies and chickens were invited to the party?

5. All the Easter bunny's cookies have been stolen! He knows that someone in his factory took them, but he isn't sure who the thief is. He asked all of them what they were doing during the time the cookies were stolen. The bunnies said they were making Easter eggs, the chickens said they were painting the Easter eggs that the bunnies had made, and the Easter bunny's assistant said that he was hiding the Easter eggs after they were painted. Which one of them is lying and took the Easter bunny's cookies?

6. It has walls of white. It is round, with a flatter bottom and a more pointed head. It's a treasure box but it doesn't have a door, key, or lid. If you manage to open this treasure box, you will find the golden treasure hidden within.

What is it?

7. You are in the Easter bunny's factory and he has asked you to make a batch of Easter chocolates. The recipe he gave you says you need 4 cups of sugar, but there's a problem. You only have two buckets, one of them measures 3 cups and the other measures 5 cups. How can you measure 4 cups of sugar using only these two buckets?

8. We are the ancient civilization in South America that gave the world the word "chocolate". We used the cacao bean to create a hot, spicy drink that we called "xocoatl" which translates in English as chocolate.

FUN FACT

Do you know what you can't do at Easter? If you live in Germany, you are banned from dancing in public on Good Friday. Up until 2018 in Ireland it was illegal to sell alcohol on Good Friday.

Ireland
up until 2018,
illegal to sell alcohol
on Good Friday

Germany
banned from
dancing in public
on Good Friday

9. The Cadbury candy company started their line of Easter candy by making smooth chocolate eggs, but soon they were making chocolate eggs with me engraved on the side. I am a plant that blooms in the spring; people often pick me and put me in vases so they can enjoy my beauty indoors.

What am I?

10. The Easter bunny needs to have 500 eggs ready in an hour so he can hide them for Easter. Let's assume that one chicken can lay 5 eggs every hour. How many chickens will the Easter bunny need so that he will have 500 eggs in an hour?

11. We are the ancient South American civilization that discovered chocolate. I think we should be known for our chocolate, but, in 2012 we were well known for our calendar, for we didn't bother to go past 2012. The Aztecs had to trade with us to get their cacao; we could grow cacao trees on our lands but on their lands they could not. They may have made it famous, but we had it first.

Who are we?

Chapter 3 - Questions

12. The Easter bunny's wife is baking cookies for the Easter bunny to eat after he is done hiding all the eggs. She has 30 cookies in the oven and the recipe says that for each cookie in the oven, add 2 minutes on to the 10-minute baking time. How many minutes should she put on the timer so she can make sure the cookies are perfect?

13. Each year Christmas falls on December 25, New Year's on January 1, Valentine's on February 14, St. Patrick's Day on March 17, and Halloween on October 31. What calendar day does Easter fall on?

Chapter 3 - Questions

14. The Easter bunny eats so much chocolate that he has become really fat. His assistant told him that he must lose some weight before next Easter; otherwise, he won't be able to hide any Easter eggs. The Easter bunny decided to do this by jogging up and down the stairs in his factory. He started on the fourth floor and jogged up five stories, he then jogged back down seven stories, he went back up six stories, jogged down another three stories, and finally jogged back up four stories. What floor did the Easter bunny end up on when he was done?

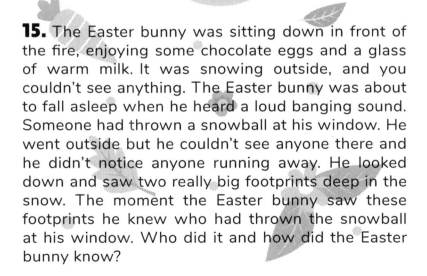

15. The Easter bunny was sitting down in front of the fire, enjoying some chocolate eggs and a glass of warm milk. It was snowing outside, and you couldn't see anything. The Easter bunny was about to fall asleep when he heard a loud banging sound. Someone had thrown a snowball at his window. He went outside but he couldn't see anyone there and he didn't notice anyone running away. He looked down and saw two really big footprints deep in the snow. The moment the Easter bunny saw these footprints he knew who had thrown the snowball at his window. Who did it and how did the Easter bunny know?

16. If you put them together, the Easter bunny and his assistant have a combined weight of 280 pounds. If the Easter bunny weighs three times as much as his assistant, how much does the Easter bunny's assistant weigh?

17. It rained all day on Easter day and a little girl put a jar outside so she could catch some of the rainwater. It was raining so hard that the jar filled up in a minute. The jar measures one cup. If she leaves it out for an hour, emptying the water into a bucket every minute, how much rainwater will she catch?

Chapter 3 - Questions

18. The Easter bunny is out hiding eggs with his two assistants. They have to keep track of time, so they don't stay out too late. They all have a watch but only one of their watches is on time. The other two are a little behind or a little ahead. The Easter bunny's watch says the time is 11:00. One of his assistant's watches says the time is 11:20. The other assistant's watch says that the time is 10:50. Which one of them has the correct time?

19. Did you know that not all societies in the world celebrate Easter on "Easter" Sunday; some people have a different day. Blame it on me. Currently, each trip around the sun I am off from reality by eleven seconds. That's not much, but it adds up.

What am I?

20. There stands a pear tree in the Easter bunny's backyard. There were twelve pears on the tree. Twelve bunnies hopped on by. Each took a pear and then left eleven pears hanging there. How is it possible that Each took a pear but there are still eleven pears left on the tree?

21. The Easter bunny fell off a roof and broke his leg the other day. He went to the hospital on Monday, November the 1st. He left the hospital on November the 30th. What day of the week was it when he left the hospital?

22. The Easter Bunny does not go to Australia; instead, I handle the holiday chores. On first glance, I may look like a rabbit, but I am not one. I am on the endangered species list. To hear my name, you might think I am William B.

Who am I?

Chapter 3 - Questions

23. You've been given a treasure map to help you find where all your Easter eggs are hidden. The only problem is that the treasure map is filled with riddles that you must solve.

Riddle 1: You will find me swimming with the fish in seawater surrounded by glass.

Riddle 2: I am lying in a thick green patch and you'll have to crawl in to find me.

Riddle 3: It smells where I am, but at least I'm behind and not beside the source of the smell.

Riddle 4: It rains where I am, but not all the time. I hope no one turns the rain on while I'm in here.

Can you solve all the riddles and find where all 4 Easter eggs are hiding?

24. The Easter bunny and his wife are out at an Ice-cream bar on a date. They both order a bowl of ice-cream with their own number of scoops in each bowl. The Easter bunny's wife says that if he gives her one of his scoops, she will have twice as many scoops as him. The Easter bunny says that if she gave him one of her scoops, they will have the same number of scoops. How many scoops do they each have?

25. If a red house is made out of red bricks, a yellow house is made out of yellow wood, and a grey house is made out of grey concrete, then what is the Easter bunny's house made out of?

26. Here is a riddle that seems like it came from the Easter Bunny's friend, the White Rabbit from Wonderland. How do you answer this? What has four letters, sometimes has nine letters, occasionally has twelve letters, always has six letters, and never has five letters. **(Hint: It has two letters.)**

Chapter 3 - Questions

27. The Easter bunny often has eggs left over after Easter and he goes down to the Easter Market to sell them before they go bad. He has a basket full of eggs. One person buys half the eggs in his basket plus half an egg. A second person buys half the eggs left in his basket plus half an egg. The third person buys half of the remaining eggs plus half an egg. The Easter bunny has now sold all his Easter eggs without needing to break a single egg. How was it done and how many eggs did the Easter bunny have to begin with?

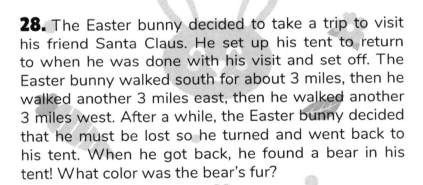

28. The Easter bunny decided to take a trip to visit his friend Santa Claus. He set up his tent to return to when he was done with his visit and set off. The Easter bunny walked south for about 3 miles, then he walked another 3 miles east, then he walked another 3 miles west. After a while, the Easter bunny decided that he must be lost so he turned and went back to his tent. When he got back, he found a bear in his tent! What color was the bear's fur?

29. Like most citizens of the year 100, the Easter Bunny shopped in the Roman marketplace for his eggs to dye for the children. As he approached a farmer, the farmer asked, "How many crates of eggs today, sir?" The Easter Bunny held up two fingers to let him know he wanted two crates. The farmer gave him five crates. Why?

FUN FACT

Do you know that if you lived in Sweden you wouldn't have an Easter Bunny? Instead in Sweden they celebrate Easter with an Easter Wizard!

30. The Easter Bunny offered to give eggs to kids on the farm, but the kids showed no interest, turned away, said "bah!", and went about their daily routine. Why weren't the kids interested in the Easter eggs?

Chapter 3 - Answers

1. The Easter bunny's assistant must put away 300 eggs. So, he must go and find the eggs that he lost and put them away.

2. Stop imagining you're in the situation!

3. Turn around and run in a circle the opposite way the thief is running. We know that the thief can only run in a circle, so if you run in a circle as well, but run the opposite way, then you will eventually run straight into the thief. Think of it as if it were two balls circling a drain. If they are going the same way, then the one ball will never catch up with the other ball. If you turn the other ball around, then the two balls will circle the drain until one runs into the other. Therefore, you can get your eggs back from the thief by running in a circle like the thief but in the opposite direction.

4. The Easter bunny invited 10 bunnies and 10 chickens to his party. The bunnies were supposed to bring 5 Easter eggs each and we know there are 50 Easter eggs at the party, so we divide the number of eggs at the party by the number of eggs each bunny was supposed to bring. If we do that, we get 10 bunnies at the party. We do the same with the chickens. We know there are 20 glasses of milk at the party and each chicken was supposed to bring 2 glasses with them. We divide the number of glasses at the party by the number of glasses each guest was supposed to bring, and we get the number of chickens at the party: 10 chickens.

5. The Easter bunny's assistant is the one lying, and he is the one who stole the cookies. He couldn't have been hiding the Easter eggs because that is the Easter bunny's job.

6. It is an egg. The golden treasure is the yolk inside.

Chapter 3 - Answers

7. There are two different ways for you to measure out 4 cups of sugar:

First: Fill the bucket that measures 3 cups up with sugar and empty that into the 5-cup bucket. Now you must fill the 3-cup bucket up again and pour some of that sugar into the 5-cup bucket until it is full. Now you have 1 cup of sugar in the 3-cup bucket. Empty out the 5-cup bucket and pour the 1 cup of sugar into it. Now fill the 3-cup bucket again and you have 4 cups of sugar. You have 1 cup of sugar in the 5-cup bucket and you have 3 cups of sugar inside the 3-cup bucket. Second: Fill the 5-cup bucket with sugar and pour some of it into the 3-cup bucket until it is full. You will be left with 2 cups of sugar in the 5-cup bucket. Now empty the sugar out of the 3-cup bucket and pour the 2 cups of sugar from the 5-cup bucket into the empty 3 cup bucket. Lastly, fill the 5-cup bucket with sugar again and pour some of the sugar into the 3-cup bucket until it is full. The 3-cup bucket already has 2 cups of sugar inside it so you will only be able to pour 1 cup of sugar from the full 5-cup bucket into the 3-cup bucket. When you have done that you will be left with the exact amount of sugar you need. You will have 4 cups of sugar inside the 5-cup bucket.

8. The ancient Aztecs

9. Flower

10. The Easter bunny would need 100 chickens to lay 500 eggs in an hour.

11. The ancient Mayas

12. If she needs to add 2 minutes for every cookie in the oven then we need to take the number of cookies and multiply them by 2 and we have to add that to 10. The cookies need to be in the oven for 70 minutes; 2 multiplied by thirty is 60 and add 10 to get 70 minutes.

Chapter 3 - Answers

13. It does not have a fixed day; it falls on the first Sunday after a full moon on or after the vernal equinox. In some years Easter will be in March and in other years it will be in April; it is always between March 22 and April 25.

14. The Easter bunny is now on the ninth floor of his factory.

15. The footprints in the snow were so big and so deep that only one big, fat man could have done it. That's how the Easter bunny knew that Santa Claus had thrown the snowball at his window.

16. The Easter bunny's assistant weighs 70 pounds. To figure this out you need to take their combined weight of 280 pounds and divide it by 4. We divide it by 4 because we know that the Easter bunny is 3 times heavier than his assistant, so their combined weight is the Easter bunny's assistants weight multiplied by 4. 280 pounds divided by 4 equals 70 pounds!

17. She will catch 60 cups of rain. If she catches 1 cup of rain every minute and she will have the jar out there for an hour, then she will be catching rain for 60 minutes. 1 cup a minute for 60 minutes is 60 cups.

18. The Easter bunny has the right time. One of the watches is a little behind and one of them is a little ahead, while the third is on time. The watch that reads 10:50 is a little behind, the watch that reads 11:20 is a little ahead, and the watch that reads 11:00 is the one that is on time. The Easter bunny's watch is on time.

19. The calendar. Different cultures use different calendars. People in Greece, Russia, and other East European cultures follow the Julian calendar, which is older but off from reality by 26 minutes per year, while people from West European cultures and North America use the Gregorian calendar, which is off by 11 seconds per year. Although there is a possibility that Easter will occur on the same day for all people, the date can occur as much as five weeks apart.

Chapter 3 - Answers

20. Each is the name of one of the bunnies that walked by. He was the only one that grabbed a pear so there are still eleven pears left.

21. If we count the days from November the 1st, which was a Monday, then we will find that the 30th of November will be a Tuesday.

22. Bilby.

23. Answer: **a.** Riddle 1: This egg is obviously hidden inside a fish tank. A sea made of glass with fish inside it.

                b. Riddle 2: This egg is probably hidden in a bush or a hedge.

                c. Riddle 3: This egg is hidden behind the garbage can... Gross!

                d. Riddle 4: This egg is hidden inside the shower. A place where it rains but someone must turn on the rain.

24. The Easter bunny has five scoops of ice-cream in his bowl and his wife has seven scoops of ice-cream in her bowl.

25. The Easter bunny's house is obviously made out of chocolate!

26. True; count the letters

27. The Easter bunny has 7 eggs to begin with. The first person bought half of them (half of 7 is 3 ½) plus half an egg for a total of 4 eggs. The second person bought half of what was left (there were 3 left so half of 3 is 1 ½) plus half an egg for a total of 2 eggs. The third person bought half of what was left (there was 1 left and half of 1 is ½) plus half an egg for a total of one egg.

28. The bear's fur was white, of course. The Easter bunny was visiting Santa Claus and he lives in the North Pole. The only bears you'll find at the North Pole are Polar bears and their fur is white.

29. The two fingers looked like a V, the Roman numeral five.

30. The kids were baby goats.

Did you enjoy the book?

If you did, we are ecstatic. If not, please write your complaint to us and we will make sure to fix it.

If you're feeling generous, there is something important that you can help me with – tell other people that you enjoyed the book.

Ask a grown-up to write about it on Amazon. When they do, more people will find out about the book. It also lets Amazon know that we are making kids around the world laugh. Even a few words and ratings would go a long way.

If you have any ideas or jokes that you think are super funny, please let us know. We would love to hear from you. Our email address is -

riddleland@riddlelandforkids.com

Riddleland Bonus Play

Join our **Facebook Group** at **Riddleland For Kids** to get daily jokes and riddles.

Bonus Book

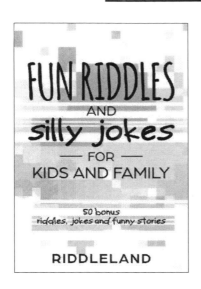

https://pixelfy.me/riddlelandbonus

Thank you for buying this book. As a token of our appreciation, we would like to offer a special bonus—a collection of 50 original jokes, riddles, and funny stories.

CONTEST

Would you like your jokes and riddles to be featured in our next book?

We are having a contest to discover the cleverest and funniest boys and girls in the world!

1) Creative and Challenging Riddles
2) Tickle Your Funny Bone Contest

Parents, please email us your child's "original" riddle or joke. **He or she could win a $25 Amazon gift card and be featured in our next book.**

Here are the rules:

1) We're looking for super challenging riddles and extra funny jokes.

2) Jokes and riddles MUST be 100% original—NOT something discovered on the Internet.

3) You can submit both a joke and a riddle because they are two separate contests.

4) Don't get help from your parents—UNLESS they're as funny as you are.

5) Winners will be announced via email or our Facebook group – Riddleland for Kids.

6) In your entry, please confirm which book you purchased.

Email us at <u>Riddleland@riddlelandforkids.com</u>

Other Fun Books by Riddleland
Riddles Series

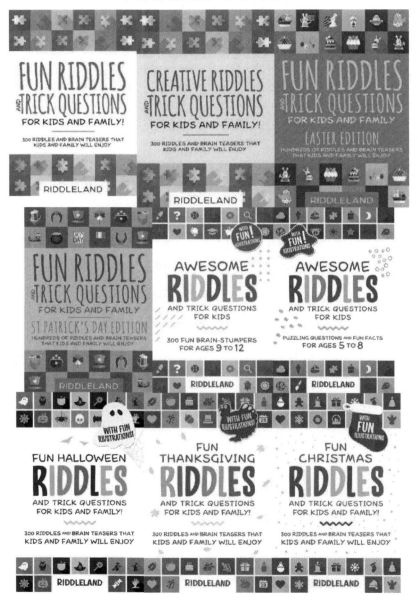

The Laugh Challenge Joke Series

Would You Rather Series

Get them on Amazon or our website at
www.riddlelandforkids.com

About Riddleland

Riddleland is a mum and dad run publishing company. We are passionate about creating fun and innovative books to help children develop their reading skills and fall in love with reading. If you have suggestions for us or want to work with us, shoot us an email a

riddleland@riddlelandforkids.com

Our family's favorite quote

"Creativity is an area in which younger people have a tremendous advantage since they have an endearing habit of always questioning past wisdom and authority."

– Bill Hewlett.

Made in the USA
Monee, IL
25 March 2021